W9-CGP-227

F/A-18E/F SUPER HORNETS

BY CARLOS ALVAREZ

BELLWETHER MEDIA · MINNEAPOLIS, MN

HAMILTON
PUBLIC
209 W. BRICK
CICERO, IN 46034

Are you ready to take it to the extreme?
Torque books thrust you into the action-packed
world of sports, vehicles, and adventure. These books
may include dirt, smoke, fire, and dangerous stunts.
WARNING: read at your own risk.

Library of Congress Cataloging-in-Publication Data

Alvarez, Carlos, 1968-
  F/A-18E/F Super Hornets / by Carlos Alvarez.
    p. cm. – (Torque: military machines)
  Summary: "Amazing photography accompanies engaging information about F/A-18E/F Super
Hornets. The combination of high-interest subject matter and light text is intended for students
in grades 3 through 7"–Provided by publisher.
  Includes bibliographical references and index.
  ISBN 978-1-60014-285-7 (hardcover : alk. paper)
  1. Hornet (Jet fighter plane)–Juvenile literature. I. Title.
  UG1242.F5A384 2010
  623.74'63–dc22

                                        2009008486

This edition first published in 2010 by Bellwether Media, Inc.

No part of this publication may be reproduced in whole or in part without written permission of
the publisher. For information regarding permission, write to Bellwether Media, Inc., Attention:
Permissions Department, Post Office Box 19349, Minneapolis, MN, 55419-0349.

Text copyright © 2010 by Bellwether Media, Inc. TORQUE and associated logos are trademarks and/or
registered trademarks of Bellwether Media, Inc.

The photographs in this book are reproduced through the courtesy of the United States Department of
Defense.

Printed in the United States of America.

Knowbuddy 14.95   10-09

CONTENTS

THE F/A-18E/F IN ACTION 4

ATTACK FIGHTER 8

WEAPONS AND FEATURES 12

F/A-18E/F MISSIONS 18

GLOSSARY 22

TO LEARN MORE 23

INDEX 24

THE F/A-18E/F IN ACTION

A **fleet** of United States warships is patrolling off an enemy coast. **Radar** shows two enemy airplanes approaching. The crew of an **aircraft carrier** springs into action.

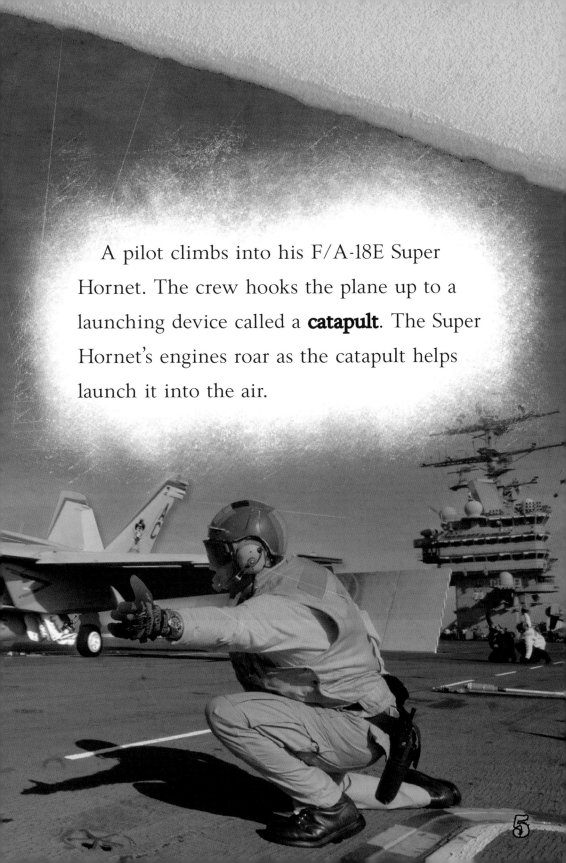

A pilot climbs into his F/A-18E Super Hornet. The crew hooks the plane up to a launching device called a **catapult**. The Super Hornet's engines roar as the catapult helps launch it into the air.

Three more Super Hornets quickly launch. They speed toward the enemy planes. One enemy plane fires a **missile**. It misses the Super Hornets. A Super Hornet fires an AIM-9 Sidewinder missile. The missile locks on to the heat of an enemy plane. It hits the plane. The plane erupts into a ball of fire. The other enemy plane retreats. The Super Hornets have completed their **mission**. The fleet is safe.

ATTACK FIGHTER

The Super Hornet is a fighter plane. It is also an attack plane. It can engage enemy planes in **dogfights**. It can also attack targets on the ground or at sea. The United States Navy uses the Super Hornet. The United States Marine Corps uses it too.

The F/A-18E/F Super Hornet first saw combat in 2002. It successfully attacked enemy aircraft in a "no fly zone" above Iraq.

The Super Hornet officially entered U.S. Navy service in 2001. The Navy uses two models of the Super Hornet. The E has one seat in the **cockpit**. The F model has two. Both models can take off from an aircraft carrier. They can also take off from a normal runway.

WEAPONS AND FEATURES

The Super Hornet is built for speed, power, and **maneuverability**. It can go faster than 1,300 miles (2,100 kilometers) per hour. Pilots can quickly change direction at high speeds. This makes the Super Hornet deadly in dogfights.

★ FAST FACT ★

The Navy is adapting the Super Hornet to make a new plane called the F/A-18G Growler. The Growler will be a radar-jamming plane.

Pilots use air-to-air missiles to destroy enemy aircraft. The AIM-9 Sidewinder is one of its best weapons. The Sidewinder is a heat-seeking missile. It locks on to the heat of an enemy plane. The AIM-120 AMRAAM is another air-to-air missile. Pilots call this radar-guided missile the "Slammer."

★ FAST FACT ★

The Super Hornet has a six-barrel M61 Vulcan cannon.
The M61 can fire 100 rounds per second.

The Super Hornet also carries bombs. It can drop them on targets on the ground or at sea. **Laser-guided bombs (LGBs)** home in on a target marked by a laser beam. SLAM missiles are controlled with small cameras. Harpoon missiles are made to destroy enemy ships. The pilot chooses the right weapon for each target.

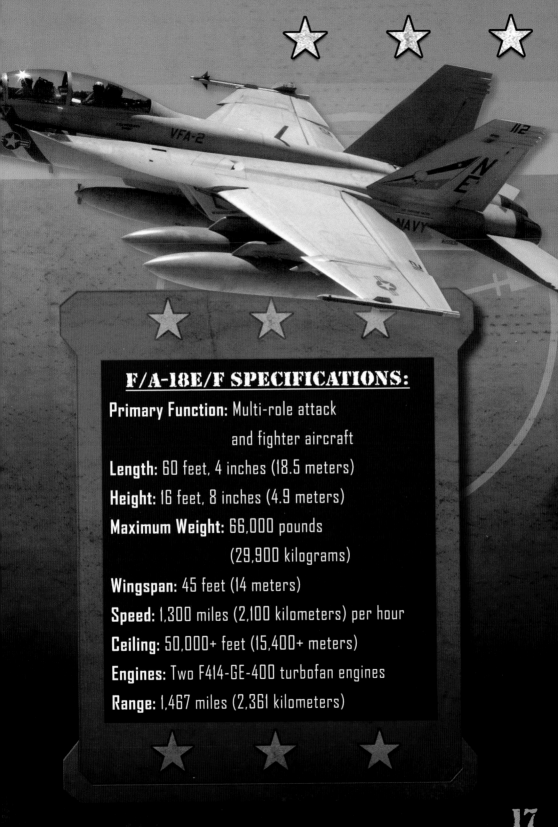

F/A-18E/F SPECIFICATIONS:

Primary Function: Multi-role attack and fighter aircraft

Length: 60 feet, 4 inches (18.5 meters)

Height: 16 feet, 8 inches (4.9 meters)

Maximum Weight: 66,000 pounds (29,900 kilograms)

Wingspan: 45 feet (14 meters)

Speed: 1,300 miles (2,100 kilometers) per hour

Ceiling: 50,000+ feet (15,400+ meters)

Engines: Two F414-GE-400 turbofan engines

Range: 1,467 miles (2,361 kilometers)

F/A-18E/F MISSIONS

The Super Hornet is a multi-task fighter. It can go on a wide variety of missions. Its main mission is to defend Navy warships. It can also go on attack missions, **escort** missions, and more. Its ability to take on many roles makes it valuable to the military.

Each Super Hornet has a pilot. The "F" model may also carry a second crew member. Groups of Super Hornets often fly in **formation**. The pilots work together to keep the fleet safe.

GLOSSARY

aircraft carrier—a huge Navy ship from which airplanes can take off and land; an aircraft carrier is like a floating airport.

catapult—a powerful launching device on aircraft carriers that helps planes gain the speed needed to take off

cockpit—the place on a plane where the pilot sits

dogfight—aerial combat between two or more fighter planes

escort—to travel alongside and protect

fleet—a group of warships

formation—a group of airplanes flying together in a set pattern

laser-guided bomb (LGB)—an explosive that locks onto a target that is marked by a laser beam

maneuverability—the ability to make quick, precise turns, especially at high speeds

missile—an explosive launched at targets on the ground or in the air

mission—a military task

radar—a sensor system that uses radio waves to detect objects

TO LEARN MORE

AT THE LIBRARY
David, Jack. *The United States Navy.* Minneapolis, Minn.: Bellwether, 2008.

Stone, Lynn M. *Super Hornet F/A-18E/F.* Vero Beach, Fla.: Rourke, 2005.

Sweetman, Bill. *Strike Fighters: The F/A-18E/F Super Hornets.* Mankato, Minn.: Capstone, 2008.

ON THE WEB
Learning more about military machines is as easy as 1, 2, 3.

1. Go to www.factsurfer.com

2. Enter "military machines" into search box.

3. Click the "Surf" button and you will see a list of related Web sites.

With factsurfer.com, finding more information is just a click away.

INDEX

AIM-9 Sidewinder, 6, 15
AIM-120 AMRAAM, 15
aircraft carrier, 4, 11
bombs, 16
catapult, 5
cockpit, 11
crew, 4, 5, 21
dogfights, 8, 12
engines, 5
escorting, 19
F/A-18G Growler, 13
fleet, 4, 6, 21
formation, 21
Harpoon missiles, 16
Iraq, 9
laser-guided bombs
  (LGBs), 16
M61 Vulcan cannon, 15
maneuverability, 12
missiles, 6, 15, 16

mission, 6, 19
models, 11
pilot, 5, 12, 15, 16, 21
radar, 4
runway, 11
SLAM missiles, 16
speed, 12
United States Marine
  Corps, 8
United States Navy, 8, 11, 19